Would you like to know

How to Pray?

by Tim Dowley
Illustrated by Eira Reeves

We all like to talk to our friends.

This book belongs to

_____

_____

and I am finding out
how to pray

Published by Candle Books
an imprint of
Lion Hudson plc
Wilkinson House, Jordan Hill Road,
Oxford OX2 8DR, England
www.lionhudson.com/candle

ISBN 978 1 78128 158 1
e-ISBN 978 1 78128 192 5

First edition 2015

A catalogue record for this book is available
from the British Library

Printed and bound in China,
October 2014, LH06

Jesus often talked to God.

We can talk to God too.
God loves us to talk to him...

and get to know him better.
Talking to God is sometimes
called praying.

You can talk to him on your own…

or with a friend…

or with a crowd of people.

God is good at listening.
He will always hear you…

wherever you are…

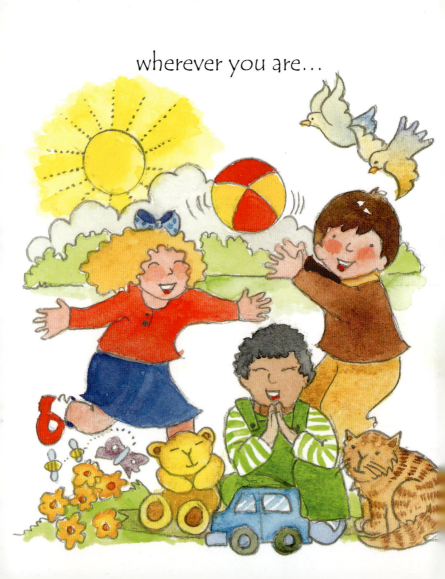

and whatever you are doing!

You can tell him if you are scared…

or sad.

He will know how you are feeling.

Tell him when you are happy too!

We can thank God for lots of things:
food…

and clothes...

and families.

When friends are ill,
we can ask him to help them.

When we have done
something wrong…

we can say sorry to him.

God listens to our prayers.

When we read our Bible
we can ask God to help us find out
what he's saying to us.

Here is a special prayer to help:
Lord God

Thank you that when I talk to you,
you always listen.

Today I want to tell you about
(use your own words here...)
Amen